TO RECEIVE ALL THAT
WE DESIRE, WE MUST
ALLOW OURSELVES
the gift of a pause.

Copyright 2025 © Adrea L. Peters and Karen P. Weaver

First published in 2025
by KMD Books
Waikiki, WA 6169

All rights reserved. No part of this book may be used or reproduced by any means, graphic, electronic, or mechanical, including photocopying, recording, taping or by any information storage retrieval system without the written permission of the copyright owner except in the case of brief quotations embodied in critical articles and reviews. Although the author and publisher have made every effort to ensure that the information in this book was correct at press time, the author and publisher do not assume and hereby disclaim any liability to any party for any loss, damage, or disruption caused by errors or omissions, whether such errors or omissions result from negligence, accident, or any other cause. This book is not intended as a substitute for the medical advice of physicians. The reader should regularly consult a physician in matters relating to his/her health and particularly with respect to any symptoms that may require diagnosis or medical attention.

Interior and cover design: Cassandra Neece

National Library of Australia Catalogue-in-Publication data:

ISBN: (hc) 978-1-7640453-2-2
ISBN: (e) 978-1-7640453-5-3
ISBN: (sc) 978-1-7640453-8-4

POWER
OF THE
PAUSE

Partnering with Silence

ADREA L. PETERS & KAREN P. WEAVER

FOUNDERS OF A&K TV

MAY YOU TRUST THE WHISPER TO
BE QUIET, CHERISH THE YET KNOWN,
AND LET ALL YOUR DREAMS

drift right to you.

TABLE OF CONTENTS

Intro ○ 8
Moments ○ 12
Cycles ○ 16
Forgets ○ 20
Voids ○ 24
Freak Outs ○ 28
Loss ○ 32
Stillness ○ 36
Relief ○ 40
Edge ○ 44
Trust ○ 48
Focus ○ 52
Align ○ 56
Reflect ○ 60
Celebrate ○ 64
Outro: A Cadenced Life ○ 68
About the Authors ○ 72
Pause for Endless Gratitude ○ 76

Intro

To pause. To stop. To let the moment pass you by—and then the next, and the next—until the silence wraps itself around you completely. Only in that stillness can you find the resonance you seek, desire, and need. The resonance you've always known was waiting for you, even if you weren't ready to admit it. Yet.

When we pause, however it comes, and don't rush to fill it with noise, something magical happens. We don't get lost in the waiting. We don't smother the precious gaps of time and space that allow things to settle and reveal what truly comes next. Instead, we recalibrate. We rediscover our course. We thrive, aligned with the deepest, most precious dreams of our hearts.

This book doesn't ask you to change. We love who you are. We love everything you accomplish, and we hope you do too. Instead, this book invites you to observe. To notice yourself in the quiet moments that life offers. To make friends with silence. To welcome it as a partner and see what unfolds.

We all go. Go! Goooo! Constantly. Often on autopilot. How could we not? There's so much to do, so many people to nurture, so many dreams to chase. The never-ending demands of life make us feel purposeful, important, as though we're truly doing something meaningful with our time. And yet, that constant motion can consume us—until we're swirling in tasks, checklists, and next steps, too busy to pause.

But here's the gift: there is no end to the demands on you. And that's a beautiful thing. No end means you get to decide. You always have. You've been making choices all along, navigating life as it unfolds. Sometimes, though, those choices come so quickly that we barely notice them. We press forward, moving through regret or hesitation with barely a second thought.

And yet, deep down, we know. A pause to let things settle could have been the best choice of all. That's why we're here—to encourage you to pause, listen, and trust yourself. Because you are the wisest voice in your life. The you within—the soul, the inner being, the quiet mentor—always knows the way.

This inner guidance never shouts. It never scolds or condemns. It whispers. It leaves breadcrumbs and drops gentle hints. It's patient, steadfast, and fully devoted to helping you succeed with love, ease, and joy. But to hear it, you have to pause. You have to give yourself space to discover how the two of you communicate.

Maybe it's through music, a song suddenly looping in your head. Maybe it's through journaling or full-blown conversations with yourself. Maybe nature sends you signs—a bird, an animal, a flower that catches your eye. However it speaks to you, pausing allows you to receive it.

In this book, we explore the many ways pausing can help you reclaim power in your life. We hope you'll feel free to open it to any page, at any time, and trust that it's the exact page you were meant to find at that moment. Consider it a little nudge from your inner self.

We know firsthand how powerful a pause can be. It's a cornerstone of our lives, something we talk about endlessly. We voice-text each other at all hours, sharing moments of pause—moments that help us reflect, connect, and grow. Between us, we've experienced every kind of pause: tiny pauses, missed pauses, needed pauses, forced pauses, and those long, soul-shifting pauses that change everything.

What we've discovered is that a pause is the most profound gift you can give yourself. It might be the only gift you ever need. And it has the power to unlock an endless cascade of blessings. When you pause—when you resist the urge to poke, prod, or over analyze a situation, response, or emotion—you create space for clarity, healing, and alignment.

We are deeply devoted to your life being more fulfilling. With all our hearts, we believe that giving yourself The Pause on a regular basis will change your life. Not just for now, but forevermore. So pause. Take a breath. Let the world settle around you. The magic is waiting.

Our hearts to yours,

Adrea & Karen

Moments

The word "please" offers a gentle pause. "Thank you" brings an even gentler one. Yet sometimes, as life speeds ahead, we forget them both. If we're feeling good, we might add them in as an afterthought. Or maybe we have a little one tugging at our sleeve to remind us, "You didn't say please or thank you!"

If this made you smile or nod, you're in the right place. This isn't about judgment or making you feel bad—it's about shining a light on one of the simplest pauses we can take. Adding a "please" or "thank you" may take just a second, but it carries a kindness that lingers. People notice when you use these words. They remember you for it. These tiny moments of acknowledgment invite stillness, a breath, a shared humanity. They're whispers of a pause—a pause that matters.

And the beauty of a pause is how easy it is to weave into your life.

We love exploring language (Adrea especially!), and the word "moment" is a treasure. On one level, it represents time—a little bit of time, a short while. As in, "Just give me a moment." Even in its essence, a moment calls forth a pause, doesn't it?

But a moment can also describe gravity—a sense of importance, whether big or small. And in physics, it represents a turning force around a pivot point, like when you push a door open. The hinges become the axis, and the moment creates movement. **A moment opens a door.**

That's the thing about moments—they gather momentum. Doors that once stood open can slam shut before you even decide whether to step through.

This is why we begin *Power of the Pause* here, with the smallest of small moments in your life. Because the smallest moments have the potential to grow—to become the largest. They can expand into something good or bad, helpful or harmful, healthy or toxic.

And before we know it, we find ourselves acting robotically, not out of intention but habit. Not because we want to, but because we're caught up in the momentum of life. The moments blend together, and we become a little numb to our own existence.

Here's the paradox, though: whether they're good or bad, **experiencing the moments of your life is deeply satisfying.** Our brains are wired to forget, so don't worry that pausing will bog you down or make life slow or mundane. Quite the opposite. Pausing helps you live in ways you never thought possible.

Micropauses—tiny, intentional moments—can transform your life. A moment to breathe. A moment to replay a sentence in your head. A moment to feel your feelings fully. Am I mad? Sad? Glad? Thrilled? Confused? A moment to pause before you respond, react, overextend, overeat, overspend, or shrink back.

A moment to stop the momentum from pulling you in the wrong direction is always worth it. When you greet a pause with intention, you steady yourself. Often, we think someone else is rushing us, but the truth is, **no one rushes you more than you do.** No one wants your dreams to succeed more than you do. And no one can claim the lead role in your life but you.

Take a moment. Just one. It might make all the difference in the world.

Cycles

A seedling begins its journey in the quiet darkness of the soil, nourished and protected until it's time to reach out into the world. Its growth unfolds slowly, in cycles, taking the time it needs.

Take a moment to think back. Whether it's your own life, the lives of your children, the animals you care for, or the ingredients you gather to prepare a feast, remember how waiting (pausing) played a role in allowing growth to happen at its own pace.

How much space do you allow for your own growth and evolution? We often rush through the process, forgetting to appreciate the nurturing, knowledge-gathering, attention, and care it takes to move forward. Life's cycles are natural, and they remind us that growth isn't always about pushing forward—sometimes, it's about slowing down.

Cycles give us time to figure out what works, and what doesn't. Rather than focusing only on new beginnings, we might benefit from asking, "How do I want this to end?" We all have moments of excitement, but often, doubt creeps into our minds, especially when we share our ideas, making us question or abandon them too soon. Your ideas are sacred. They are the seeds of your life's garden.

It's worth pausing to consider our relationship at the beginning of a cycle to develop your intention on what and why you want the promise of the idea fulfilled at the end of the cycle. Without pausing to challenge our fears, we risk letting something meaningful fade away before it has a chance to grow.

When we move through our resistance, refine our ideas, seek guidance, and accept that growth can be difficult, our ideas truly begin to flourish. Whether it's a small step like making it through today's workout or something larger like building a dream team, the process remains the same: it takes time.

Pauses are essential to the cycle. One pause might mean pushing an idea aside before giving it the love and attention it needs. Another pause could help you avoid a risky decision that saves you from hardship.

A cycle takes us from where we are to where we want to be. Embracing the pauses along the cycle lock in our ability to know what is right for us, and what is not. A pause worth its weight in gold!

forgets

We are wired to forget. Thank goodness.

Forgetting is one of the most natural, accessible pauses we have. And no, we're not talking about memory issues or medical diagnoses here, nor do we ever intend to trigger anyone navigating more serious complications with memory. That is not, and will never be, our purpose.

We're talking about the everyday forgetting we all experience. Our memories are not perfect—they are fluid, malleable, and shaped by our perceptions. Sometimes we shape them, and sometimes they seem to shape us.

But here's the thing: when we get trapped in yesterday—bullying ourselves over what went wrong, replaying moments we wish we could change—our memories can start to haunt us.

Here's the truth: **you can't change yesterday.** It's done. It's over. It's not coming back. You are free.

Of course, you can try to recreate yesterday. But why try? Why struggle to repeat an amazing day when you have the opportunity to create an even better one today? Yesterday's triumphs are now part of your story—they've already elevated you, taught you, inspired you. Celebrate that and keep moving forward!

And yes, the reverse is also true: if you let it, today could go worse than yesterday.

This is why forgetting can be a beautiful synonym for pausing. The most restorative pause of all is a fabulous night of sleep. Studies show that dreaming, whether you remember it or not, is a powerful way to release yesterday's hold on you. Sleep allows your brain to let go, to file away what matters and discard the rest. When you wake up, you're given the gift of a fresh start.

Take that moment, right there in the morning, to decide how your day will go. Set your intention. Speak it out loud. Feel it in your heart. Hands over your chest, lock it in. Choose love. Choose joy. Choose freedom.

When we cling to remembering, when we fight to recreate, we become heavy.

When we allow ourselves to forget, we become lighter, brighter, and infinitely more creative.

Forgetting shows up in small ways every day, offering us a chance to pause. Take the classic, *"Where in the world did I put that?"* Suddenly, you're in a pause. You can choose frustration—rushing and frantically searching every corner of your purse, couch, or bag—or you can choose calm. You can breathe, sit for a moment, and reconnect with intention. Ask yourself, *"Why do I need to find this? Does it really matter? What if I'm not meant to find it right now?"*

We never imagined we'd be offering up "forgetting" as a gift. And yet, here we are, celebrating the gift it brings. Forgetting lets us pause. It lets us release. It lets us reset.

So go ahead: **feel free to forget.**

Voids

Sometimes a pause is "imposed" on you.

These pauses, often seen as voids in our otherwise action-packed lives, can feel unsettling. They tend to arrive when you've done all you can in a situation or with a person, leaving you alone in that quiet, awkward space, asking yourself, *"Now what?"*

Voids are the moments after a goodbye at the end of a meal. They linger after you submit a job application, finish a heated argument, send an edgy text, or complete a project you've poured your soul into for months—or even years. They follow the vulnerable moments, those times when you put yourself out there in ways that leave your heart wide open.

And the biggest clue that you've entered a void? The flood of questions:
"Why haven't I heard back?"
"Why won't they respond?"
"What am I supposed to do now?"
"How long do I have to wait?"

Voids are deeply felt, aren't they?

Yet, one of the hardest things to do is **not fill the void** with noise. We're so used to the chaos, the movement, the endless doing that we rarely let ourselves just be. We crave peace and quiet, but the moment it arrives, we fill it. We scroll. We text. We check email for the hundredth time. We turn on the TV, do the dishes, call a friend—anything to avoid sitting with the void.

Why? Because voids can feel scary. They're uncomfortable. And we've made it a habit to do, do, do.

Try this: Count to ten—slowly, without rushing. Notice how hard it can be to even get to three without your mind jumping ahead. Now imagine that same stillness stretched out for hours, days, or weeks. That's the nature of a void.

But here's the secret: **voids are where the magic happens.**

Being okay in a void requires skill, yes, but it also requires trust—trust that not knowing what's next is okay. The void invites you to let go of certainty, to stop forcing outcomes, and to embrace the stillness. It's here, in this space of non-doing, that resilience is built. Clarity blooms. New doors quietly open.

When you allow yourself to rest in a void, miraculous things happen:

- Problems dissolve because you're not fueling them with your energy.
- Missteps are avoided.
- Fights don't start.
- Money isn't wasted impulsively.
- Opportunities reveal themselves.

We all have proof of this. Think of the times when you were too tired to respond to a situation, only to find it resolved itself without you lifting a finger. That's the power of the void.

You can train yourself to pause instead of reacting. To ask, *"What if I don't do anything right now?"* This is not about checking out—it's about checking **in.** The void is not a space of nothingness. It's a space of renewal, a place where clarity can emerge.

When you are clear, you are in your power.

Think of the void as a touchpoint, a chance to check back in with your foundation. Ask yourself:

- *Did my recent actions bring me closer to my intentions, or further away?*
- *What do I truly want to create in my life?*

In this stillness, you reconnect with your intentions:

- *I intend to be kind to myself.*
- *I intend to live with integrity.*
- *I intend to create success without compromising my values.*

Voids may take time to love, especially because they often arrive when we feel most vulnerable or uncertain. They test our trust in ourselves, our dreams, and our path. But they also invite us to recommit. In a void, you can say to yourself:

No matter what, I am committed to my dreams. I am on track. This is my time to pause, reflect, and savor how far I've come. May I be calm. May I be still. May I enjoy this moment of reprieve from all the doing.

It is in these pauses, these voids, that new paths to joy and fulfillment appear. When we stop pushing, forcing, or pulling, we make space for life to flow naturally—on time and by invitation.

So, embrace the pleasure of a good, long void. Sit with it. Let it settle into your bones. You may find yourself falling in love with the stillness, with your life as it unfolds in its own beautiful way.

Magic happens here. We promise.

freakouts

Now that we've explored the calm that a void can bring, let's also acknowledge that sometimes... everything does explode, and you might find yourself totally overwhelmed. You and your impatience leap across the void option and charge headfirst into the fire! There's truly nothing quite like the raw energy of a good freakout.

Why? Because it's fueled by passion. When you're deeply invested in something, you care enough to feel that intensity. Passion is what makes these moments truly significant. When we're not so connected to something, we can sit in the void, wait, and let things unfold without much concern. But when you care deeply, the pause feels like a threat, and that's when the freakout happens.

It's a sign that you care. When something that matters to you seems to be slipping away, falling apart, or just not going as planned, you fight for it. Even if deep down, you know it might be time to let go, in the heat of the moment, all you can do is lose it. And you should. What matters to you deserves your full attention and energy. So, let yourself have that moment. Don't hold back.

But remember: this isn't about taking it out on anyone else. Never. Do no harm. Not to them, and especially not to yourself. Let others feel however they feel about your reaction, but know that this is *your* process.

Your freakout is between you and you. No one else.

It can feel like it's someone else's fault, that they somehow caused this storm inside you. But in truth, what you care about may not matter in the same way to anyone else, and that's okay. That's actually beautiful. You are the keeper of your dreams, the one who gets to decide what matters most.

And eventually, you will run out of steam. All storms eventually calm. Not only did you express your passion, but you also learned to ground yourself and realize that you are okay. This is a powerful journey of growth. Pay attention to the bravery you're building, and the next time a setback comes your way, you might find yourself handling it with more grace.

We hope you have someone to lean on when you're in that space. When we freak out, we remind each other things like, "Wow, I'm so glad you care so much about this. It shows how much it matters to you." Or, "This is a moment of clarity. Can you see how strong you are? Look how far you've come!" Over time, we've learned that freakouts aren't failures—they're opportunities to step back, breathe, and gain a new perspective on what's happening.

When someone is there to help you calm down, it can be so soothing that it makes the whole freakout feel worth it. We're not saying that freaking out is ideal, but sometimes it's the only way to see clearly what really matters to you. Sometimes, everything has to fall apart before you can put it back together in a stronger way. Investing in yourself is powerful.

Loss

There are moments when the pause comes after something—or someone—has moved on. Maybe it's a person, a loved one, a mentor (even if you never met them), a job, a career, a home, an office, or a place that held meaning. Whatever it is, you realize that you can no longer hold onto what once was. It is gone. Physically, at least.

And in that moment, the pause begins.

It's never wrong to mourn a loss. In fact, it's necessary. Can you give yourself the space to grieve? Please, don't rush past this part. Don't move on before you've allowed yourself to truly feel it. We're not grief experts, but we want to remind you that life after loss calls for a pause.

You need time to regroup and reflect on how this loss has affected you. Let it become a part of your story, your purpose, your legacy. More than just a freakout or a void, loss opens the door to a deeper understanding of what really matters to you. **When something or someone is gone, that emptiness is real, and it's time to sit with it.** It takes time and energy to understand what's next. If you can, try to welcome the light that shines through that emptiness as you settle into the pause.

In that light, you'll have a chance to reconsider your intentions. Does this still matter? Who would I be if this were no longer part of my life? What do I truly want moving forward? Who am I at my best? What does that version of me look like, sound like, act like? Can I be brave enough to step into that person? Can I trust this loss to help me grow?

There's no need to rush. No need to hurry or push. Let yourself fully feel the weight of the loss. Take the time to breathe in what nourishes your soul. And let the light that comes from this experience guide you toward where you need to go next.

Life has a way of shifting entirely after loss. In those moments of pause, we are not being asked to stop living—we are being invited to reflect, to gently examine all that surrounds us. Both of us have felt the pain of profound loss, and we understand how slow and heavy progress can feel in its aftermath. Time seems to stand still, the walls close in, and for a while, even the beauty of the world may lose its meaning.

But slowly, ever so gently, we rebuild. Bit by bit, step by step, we move forward. We make promises to ourselves—some we honor, others we release. And in the process, we are given a gift: the ability to pay closer attention to life's small, precious moments. Loss teaches us that endings are inevitable, that everything eventually finds its close.

The question then becomes not what will end, rather, what will you choose to begin?

Stillness

The very *sound* of the word makes us pause. It beckons us to close our eyes and sink into ourselves. It's the most soothing, peaceful word we know. It halts us in our tracks and invites us to exhale with relief.

It's a word from within, not from the outside. Inclusive, not exclusive. Full of emotion, courage, and clarity. It wraps around you like a gentle, powerful hug and holds you in a space of love and calm. Stillness is a best friend, always ready to show up with exactly what you need.

Can you sit with stillness, or does it slip away from you? As we write this, it's hard to keep our eyes open because Stillness is so *quietly* overwhelming in its presence. It carries Intention—it knows exactly who it is, and it wants to gift you that same knowing.

But stillness isn't always easy. It can feel harder than chaos, fear, or uncertainty. Stillness asks only one thing of us: to simply be. No thoughts, no plans, no analysis—just being. It's a fleeting moment, yes, but one so potent it can shift everything. A single moment of stillness is a powerful pause—one that can change the tone of your day or even the trajectory of your life.

Meditation is where stillness is allowed to take the lead. The masters of stillness can free themselves entirely, even from thought. We aren't there yet—and that's okay. One moment of stillness is plenty.

When we're able to let one moment of stillness flow into the next, something magical happens: stillness begins to rewire our inner world. It helps us shift from chaos to calm, from panic to peace. It becomes a tool to prevent spirals, both big and small. If we allow it, stillness can even become an action—a way of living.

Picture a moment of nothingness. You're in the kitchen, the garage, the bathroom, or your car. You're safe. You're okay. You inhale the goodness surrounding you, hold it for a heartbeat, and let it fill every corner of your being. Then, you exhale—releasing tension, clutter, stress—watching it drift away like particles carried far from you.

In that instant, you are still. You are free.

Relief

Relief comes when we let go—when we loosen our grip on the game, the fight, the push and pull, and the endless "on" of life. Relief feels like a long, slow exhale, stretched out like soft taffy, gently pulling us toward relaxation—of the mind, the body, and the noise that surrounds us.

Relief often follows moments that have stirred us up. Anxiety, stress, pain, sadness, despair, grief, confusion, hurt—we all know these feelings more intimately than we'd wish. And while we may want to push them down, suppressing what we feel only forms knots within us, tangles that can take a lifetime to loosen. We all understand the weight of being wound too tightly.

So, we ask you gently: Are you finding relief? Are you creating space for it, allowing a pause to guide you toward release and relaxation? Do you feel like you are capable of giving yourself some relief from the stress and craziness?

Here's what we believe—you can give yourself relief. It's a choice. A choice you are worthy of making.

Inhale. *Exhale*. Pause. Ask yourself this: In this moment, right here and now, am I under attack? Am I being hunted, hounded, or harmed? **Relief asks us—no, it demands—that we separate from the illusions in our minds, the ones that whisper we are in danger when we are not.**

Inhale. *Exhale.* Let your shoulders drop, your breath slow, and your muscles release. Don't give power to the thoughts or opinions that say otherwise. Instead, turn away. Shift your stance. Say, no to suffering. Suffering is an opinion, not a truth. We are only meant to suffer long enough to learn that it doesn't serve us.

Take a moment to thank your stress for what it has tried to show you, but let it go with gratitude. Remind yourself of the beauty you are creating in your life, the richness that surrounds you, the gratitude that fills your heart. Relief is not just a sensation—it's profound knowing that you are alive, here, and deserving of peace.

Say it to yourself: *I am not meant to suffer longer than necessary to remind me of how extraordinary my life is. Stress is only a signal—a reminder that I am veering into thoughts or beliefs that do not serve me. I choose relief. I choose to thrive. I choose to embrace my unique path and let love flow to me and through me.*

Feel the threads of stress transform into threads of relief, rippling through you like waves, carrying you toward relaxation and release. Let yourself float in the truth of your well-being. Relief is here, always within reach, waiting for you to pause and claim it.

Edge

We absolutely *love* the word *edge*. Sit with it for a moment. Say it out loud: Edge. Edge. Edge. Feel its energy, its sharpness, its potential.

Edge of what? Edge to where? Let's explore.

Aren't we always on the edge of something? When we slow life down—like a slow-motion replay—we can see it so clearly. We're always on the edge of the next thought, the next feeling, the next decision, the next step.

And in that space, right there on the edge, there's an opening. A chance to pause before our thoughts tumble forward into a thunderous crescendo of negativity or doubt.

Do you see why we adore this word? *Edge* holds so much power. It's a reminder that, with a moment of awareness, you can slip in a positive thought—a kinder thought—before a not-so-great one takes hold. And in that instant, everything shifts. In that snap, you pivot toward your dreams, your intentions, your deepest desires, and your life's purpose.

Have you ever considered that whatever you're thinking or doing right now—*in this very moment*—is the purpose of your life? We first heard this concept from the great Byron Katie, who taught that life unfolds only in the present. Whatever you're engaged with now is your life's purpose because now is all we have. Yesterday is gone—it's a memory, not a place we can live. And isn't that freeing? Isn't that powerful?

This doesn't mean we should never look back or stroll down Memory Lane. Reminiscing is a joy! But we must remember that being "stuck" is just a thought—a momentary opinion about where we are. If you dig in and convince yourself you're stuck, you'll feel stuck because your thoughts are *that* powerful.

But here's the beauty: you have the edge. You know better. You can see this moment for what it is—a pause, an opportunity, a choice.

The edge is where you stop the spiral of negative, fearful, or troubling thoughts before they gain momentum. It's where you step back, breathe, and reverse into the positive. Let the edge be your guide, the nudge that propels your life forward.

Ask yourself:

- "Is it really that bad?"
- "How true is this for me?"
- "What if I saw this differently?"
- "How can I soften this opinion?"
- "What do I really want?"
- "What truly matters to me?"
- "What do I need right now?"

The edge is a pause that can transform everything in an instant. It can shift you from uncertainty to clarity, from fear to freedom, from resistance to ease. The edge lets you swap frustration for joy, doubt for confidence, and hate for love.

You *have* the edge. You are moving toward your dreams, one thoughtful pause at a time.

ADREA L. PETERS & KAREN P. WEAVER

Trust

The power of trust is truly extraordinary. Trust in what? Simply *trust*. Not trust in someone or something external, but trust as a way of being—a foundation that starts within.

Do you trust yourself? It's a big, vulnerable question, isn't it? Take your time with it. We are deeply trusting souls—and yes, at times, we've been burned. Why? Because we gave our trust away. We believed others knew better than we did, whether out of fear, doubt, or simply wanting to please. But when we hand over the power of trust to someone else, life gently (or not-so-gently) teaches us the lesson we need most: to trust ourselves.

You are never alone. You always have the best partner of all: your bright, beautiful soul.

Think of your soul as the highest version of you. That energy within you that knows your truth. It holds you, guides you, and loves you unconditionally—no matter what you've done or who you've hurt. Your soul doesn't judge. It whispers gently, offering guidance, answers, and clarity. But to hear it, you must pause, quiet the noise, and truly listen.

Trust anchors you to the best of you. It keeps you rooted in who you truly are and aligns you with what you truly want. **Your soul isn't separate from you; it *is* you.** Trust is the bridge that connects you to yourself. And the more you fine-tune that connection, the stronger your trust becomes—unshakable and absolute.

Trust is also a practice—a single, steady master. It invites you to pause and ask, "Is this right for me? Is this the next step I want to take?" The more connected you are to yourself, the faster those answers come. But remember, this isn't a race. It's a journey, a practice ground where every stumble is an opportunity to grow.

And yes, you'll make mistakes. You'll leap when you should've paused, and you'll think, "I *knew* it. I should've listened to myself." But those moments are gifts—they teach you. Each time you fall and rise again, your trust muscles strengthen. Each "I knew it!" is clarity earned, another layer of self-awareness.

If you're one of those enthusiastic, jump-right-in souls, we see you. We *are* you. And we love that about you. But even the boldest hearts need to build trust within. Pause. Listen to yourself. Let your inner voice guide you before you leap.

This practice of pausing to trust yourself might just be the most powerful move you'll ever make. It's how you create a life built on clarity, alignment, and love—a life where you are truly in partnership with your soul.

focus

We want to share our take on the magic life force that is focus. At first glance, pause and focus might not seem as wonderful a couple as they are. Yet when you focus for a moment, are you not in a pause? For us, it is you in your zone. It doesn't matter what you are focused on, only that you are focused. Stay with us here... when you focus, even on a television program, and you are fully into it, listening to the dialog, watching every scene, enveloped in the plot, are you not pausing everything else? Hmmm. Something to consider.

When you are thinking about a thousand and one other things, that is not focus. That's a mind mayhem. Which is something you might need at that moment. Scatter to focus. That is a natural progression. Moment by moment, lock in focus on whatever you are doing or opinionating and try to hold it on one thing at a time. We do not mean don't multitask. Go for it. To us, multitasking is the autobahn of focus. Micro-tasking might be a better name for it. You focus on one micro thing then move to the next. It is incredibly satisfying. Box ticking makes us all shine!

Focus, like most things, is a skill. We believe anything can be learned. You are limitless. One thousand percent limitless. To know that, to own it, to possess that fearless flow of everything you desire, crave, seek and long for coming to you, you need to master your focus. And when we are fully focused, we are actually, technically, and wonderfully, in a Pause. How incredible is that?

Being in focus is being clear and being relaxed. You know what you need to do and you are doing it. As we write each chapter, as we talk through this book, as we WhatsApp endlessly about the Power of the Pause, we are so freaking focused that the distance between our houses evaporates completely and we are in the same room, side by side, in flow and in focus. There is no time or space separation. There is no limitation to how great we create. There is us and our combined focus on you and the words we chose to put to the page. It is a true delight. Nothing else matters. Nothing else exists. It's you and us, enraptured in a pause, filled with focus.

We want to say it's simple. It will be. Give yourself the grace of ease and belief that you can focus. Ask others in your home/work to give you a few minutes to focus. Schedule focus time and actually focus on one thing at a time. The time you give your focus may last days, months, years, decades, lifetimes, or it can last less than a second.

A kiss. Focus on it. A bite of food. Focus. Someone speaking to you. Focus on them so you can hear and absorb what they are saying. Catch yourself looking at their facial features or wardrobe and FOCUS on what they are saying. A thought. Focus on it as an opinion and decide if it serves your intentions. If not, let it go and focus on a thought that does serve your intentions. These initial micro-focus moments will train you for more focus. Start small. Dream big. Repeat.

Let focus be your superpower and superpartner and watch what unfolds effortlessly before you.

Align

We can't pretend otherwise—the pause that comes when everything aligns is pure gold. When the pieces of life's puzzle fall effortlessly into place, and you can see, feel, taste, touch, and fully experience them—it's fulfillment in its most radiant form.

However, alignment doesn't always arrive in an instant. We know this. There are seeds we planted years—lifetimes—ago that have yet to bloom. The key is not getting lost in the waiting or abandoning your dream altogether. Moving from one thing to the next without pausing to ask, *Does this align with what I truly want?* can leave you feeling unsatisfied, over-compromised, and disconnected from the life you've envisioned.

We've all been there—settling for "close enough" or "good enough." But here's the truth: you deserve more than that. The pause to align with your true intentions, dreams, and desires is everything. Yes, there will be times to compromise, and that's okay. Take those partial wins with grace and gratitude, but never lose sight of your greater vision. The dream lives on because you live on—and you deserve it all and more.

Sometimes, what feels like alignment in the moment turns out to be a stepping stone rather than the destination. And that's okay too. Every experience you embrace, when aligned with who you are at the time, is valuable. Life shifts, circumstances change, and people grow in unexpected ways. But taking a moment to pause, check in, and ask, *Does this truly align with my intention?*

is an act of self-honoring courage. **Saying, "No, this doesn't align, and that's okay," can be as liberating as saying yes to what does.**

We want opportunities to come to you in waves, and in abundance. And you already hold the tools to discern what is meant for you. Your body is a remarkable tuning fork for alignment. How do I feel? Does this feel light, expansive, and empowering? Or heavy, restrictive, and uneasy? Your mind will have opinions, and your body will translate them into feelings and sensations. Trust those signals. No one else can tell you what alignment looks like for you—only *you* can know.

If you're still exploring what alignment means for you, start here: How do you feel as you read these words? Are you nodding, smiling, highlighting, or sharing? Are you frustrated, annoyed, or uplifted? Your reactions are a powerful guide. Pausing to check in—*Aligned or not?*—is the process that will take you closer to your truth.

And what about the things you're currently doing that don't feel aligned? Maybe you can't immediately walk away for practical or emotional reasons. Some of life's greatest lessons come from moments of misalignment—they help us better understand ourselves. Those experiences are teachers. They bring clarity, and with clarity comes freedom.

You don't need to run from the life you're living. Life is a gift, even in its messiest moments. What you need is to align yourself with the life you desire, one thoughtful pause at a time. Let the life you want come into being—it's waiting for you, always.

Reflect

This might be one of the most natural pauses to recognize. Reflection invites us to pause instinctively, leaning back in a gesture of release and introspection. It's like glancing over your shoulder at what just unfolded, allowing yourself a moment to let it all sink in. Reflection is a gift—a chance to acknowledge what went well, what could have gone better, and what may have fallen to pieces. It's a sacred moment between you and yourself, and sometimes shared with others, to lovingly gaze upon the moments that shaped your yesterday. What a beautiful pause to take.

Through reflection, we honor our yesterdays with care and intention. It's a time to gather the pieces, cherish the lessons, and decide what to carry forward. We get to choose what reflects who we are today—what aligns with the person we've become after navigating life's triumphs and trials. It takes courage to pause and reflect, to sift through the moments and decide what to keep and what to release, letting it fade into the distance like a soft memory.

The serenity of reflection is profound and transformative. Yet, so much of what we hear about "not looking back" can feel confusing. It's true—you can't fix yesterday. What happened, happened. Be honest about it, without judgment. The good, the bad, the messy—it all deserves to be seen. Pause and let it sink in. Find the lesson, discover the meaning, and carry that wisdom forward.

When we rush through life, we often miss these moments of reflection. Rest assured, life has a way of bringing the lessons we need back to us, again and again, until we take notice. **The more we embrace the pause to reflect, the less we'll need to repeat the same patterns that no longer serve us.**

Reflection doesn't have to be about monumental moments—it can arise from the small things, too. Maybe you notice you've been short-tempered, easily triggered, or overly self-critical when a particular situation arises or when someone behaves in a certain way. We all have these moments. The next time it happens, pause to reflect. *Why does this upset me so much? Why do I keep putting myself in this situation? Why is it so hard to let this go?* Let those questions guide you. You may not always trace the exact root of the discomfort, and that's okay. Knowing it's there is enough to start.

Use the pause to decide who you want to be. What parts of yourself do you want to reflect onto others? Sometimes, being firm and setting boundaries is the truest reflection of who you are. Other times, softness and grace hold the answer. The key lies in the pause—giving yourself the time and space to choose.

What you reflect out into the world is reflected back to you. Life and the people in it serve as mirrors, showing you the energy and intentions you've put forth. Does that not make it worth pausing to craft the reflection you desire? You have the power to decide, to create, and to reflect the truest, most aligned version of yourself. Take the pause. It's where transformation begins.

Celebrate

There is no pause more exhilarating—or easier to take—than the pause to celebrate! And yet, so often, it's rushed through, skipped over, or given only a fleeting second before we move on to the next thing.

Let's stop doing that. Right now. Please.

Celebrate! Take the time to pause and say, "Wait a second—I did that!" "Look at what we accomplished!" "Wow, I actually did it!" These moments are precious, and we need to savor them. In fact, we often say to each other, "Let's take a moment to celebrate this." And you know what? You can even celebrate the missteps and the things that didn't go as planned—with humor and grace. A little laugh, like, "Whoops! That didn't work!" or "Well, now we know what not to do!" or "Did I seriously just say that?" can turn a stumble into a stepping stone. As long as you catch yourself before any negativity takes root, you can celebrate the knowledge gained and keep moving forward with lightness.

The energy of celebration is what truly matters.

It's light. It's expansive. **It's an enchanting pause where you recognize yourself as triumphant, as a success, as someone who is fully participating in the creation of their own life.** And why is this so important? Because it's too easy to forget. These moments of celebration remind you that you are successful, you are triumphant, and you are worthy of everything you desire.

To celebrate is to mark a moment—a completion of something meaningful, big or small. It's owning your role in your own journey. And please don't dismiss mistakes as unworthy of celebration. Every mistake teaches you something invaluable. The more you understand what doesn't work, the more clearly you see what does. And the more you celebrate what's working, the more aligned and confident you become.

When we pause to celebrate, we're saying, "YES! I belong here! I belong in this moment of joy, this dream, this life I've created!"

But here's the truth—it's all too easy to breeze past these pauses. We know this because we've been guilty of it ourselves. And now, we're committed to doing better. We're committed to celebrating, truly and fully. And we invite you to join us in this commitment.

You deserve a plan to celebrate. You deserve moments to shine and glow. You deserve to feel the weight of how far you've come and the excitement of how far you're going. Because you belong in your dream life. It's yours, and yours alone, to celebrate—over and over again.

So take that bow. Pause. Celebrate. Glow.

We love you, and we're celebrating you, always!

Outro
A Cadenced Life

Congratulations on making it through all that pausing! Was that the longest you've ever paused? Maybe! It certainly was for us. Isn't it amazing what unfolds when we tap into the power of the pause? We hope, by now, you're beginning to see just how transformative pausing can be—how it puts you firmly in the driver's seat of your life.

The journey of this book was a pause of its own. We thought about it for ages before putting pen to paper. In fact, Adrea took a big pause in 2023 that spilled into 2024. It was one of those "life's momentum isn't working." She threw her hands in the air, disengaged entirely, and gave herself space to find clarity. The stress and disappointment were too much to carry without that pause. As she emerged from her void and reached out to Karen in a meaningful way, she discovered Karen had been in a pause of her own.

And that's when it clicked. The dust settled, and *Power of the Pause* was born.

True to its name, this book didn't come together immediately. Oh no—we had plenty of freakouts, voids, and cycles before we really committed to its creation. As writers, we live in the space of ideas before putting them on the page. We think, we ponder, we toss concepts back and forth, letting them simmer and shift until they resonate. That's our process. We trust the pause. We start. We pause. We evaluate. We talk. We reflect. We let our ideas breathe, and only then do we move forward with clarity and intention.

This book was no different. We set out to create a "pause vocabulary"—a language to help you see the possibilities and gifts that silence holds. Silence doesn't need to be feared or rushed through. Instead, it can be embraced, partnered with, and cherished as a guide to deeper insight and alignment.

As we approached the finish line, something interesting happened. Adrea took stock of the selected words and felt one needed to go. She didn't know why, but she trusted her gut. She paused, counted, and realized there were 14 words left. And as it turns out, 14 is magical.

We looked it up. The number 14 symbolizes balance, harmony, and commitment to your dreams. It's a sign of hope, strength, and forward momentum—encouraging calm, presence, and positivity no matter the circumstance. A divine reminder that thoughtful, deliberate pauses lead to meaningful growth and alignment. Of course, we celebrated. "Of course 14 is magical! That's exactly how our lives roll!"

And that's what we want for you—for your life to roll in alignment, with magic and joy. For your pauses to be purposeful and empowering. Weird things will happen. Missteps will occur. That's life. But with intention, you can pause, reset, and move forward—letting go of opinions and energies that no longer serve you.

From our hearts to yours, we thank you for pausing with us. We hope to see you, hear from you, and celebrate with you as you create a new, beautiful relationship with The Power of the Pause.

Here's to all the magic that lies ahead!

With love,

Adrea & Karen

ABOUT ADREA

Adrea Peters is a storyteller, weaving tales that dive deep into love, logic, wellbeing and human potential. Her mission? To remind you that you are the hero of your life's story. A valedictorian with a journalism degree from the University of Colorado at Boulder, she later earned a Master's in Popular Fiction Writing from Seton Hall University.

Her impressive body of work spans novels, screenplays, and articles. *The Becoming Truitt Skye* trilogy marked her fiction debut in 2020. Bestselling *Quantum Thinking* offers powerful affirmations to unlock your potential.

Adrea's collaborative spirit shines through transformative works like *When I Go Outside, I Go Inside* with Teffanie Thompson and *Quantum Wealth* with Amber Lilyestrom. Adrea and publishing powerhouse Karen Weaver co-host the groundbreaking A?K TV and together they crafted *Quantum Love* in 2021. The two's long-awaited release of *The Power of the Pause* will be released in 2025. Notably, *Quantum Thinking* and *When I Go Outside, I Go Inside* were in the 2021 Academy Award gift bags.

A mentor for over three decades, Adrea fuels the growth of writers with her workshops and her award-winning book, *The Science of Story*. Recognized as one of Brainz Magazine's Top 500 Entrepreneurs, she's set to be honored at the Women Changing the World Global Awards this May. She is also a featured speaker and writer in the *Hear Us Roar* docufilm and book series releasing multiple times throughout 2025.

Adrea loves connecting! Please stop by adreapeters.com and @adreapeters2025 and send her a message!

OTHER TITLES BY ADREA

ABOUT KAREN

Karen Weaver is a visionary author, accomplished publisher, and life philosopher known for her profound insights into mindfulness, knowing, intention, love, gratitude, forgiveness, and belief. With a remarkable career spanning various genres, including novels, motivational literature, children's books, and journals, she has consistently led the way in her authorship, generously sharing her transformative philosophies through the power of the written word.

Her work transcends traditional literary boundaries, offering profound wisdom and guidance in diverse facets of life. In addition to her prolific writing career, Karen has emerged as a prominent figure in the publishing world. Having built a highly successful publishing empire from the ground up, she has nurtured major authors, authored over 40 impactful books, and established her own credible brand in the market. Her innovative strategies and techniques are anchored in the power of "Knowing" to manifest dreams and aspirations into reality.

OTHER TITLES BY KAREN

   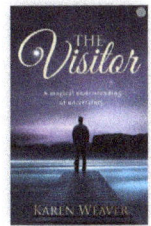

PAUSE FOR OUR ENDLESS GRATITUDE

Thank you, dear reader! Without you, we wouldn't be doing this! You are everything to us! Endless thank you to each and every one of you!

Cass! You've done it again! You are such an incredible genius. You brought this book to life with your incredible design work. We are in utter awe of your talent and want to express our deepest gratitude to you. Thank you, dear soul. Thank you!

Big, giant, bold love from Adrea to...

Karen Weaver! I am so endless grateful that you wanted to create this beautiful and important book together. Our synthesis and connectedness is otherworldly and it pleases me every single day! You always make me smile and fill my heart with pure joy. I treasure that I get to work with you, Karen! Thank you!

Scott Peters, the best brother a sister could ever ask for! You probably don't even know I'm writing this! And it doesn't matter. Your support of me in all ways is the bees knees. No one makes me laugh like you do. No one knows me like you do. Thank you for being such a huge, important part of my life. I would not be me if not for you. Thank you.

Nikki Krout. You know why. You, you are everything. Start to finish. No one sees me like you do, and I will never be able to thank you enough for it. Yet. I will continue to try forevermore. xoxo I love you!

Magical thank yous all around from Karen to...

My kids! Life is complete because of you all! Who would of known that 6 humans could come out of the same person and yet be so different! You each stand tall, strong and courageous in your individual knowing and dreams for your future. I love you all with all of my heart. Thank you for choosing me to be your mum!

Adrea! We did it! I love how we both harmonise and be! Even the bumps felt like they had a deep profound knowing driving them. Our connection transcends quantum fields! I appreciate you and your genius, more than you will ever know. The world needs your genius guiding it. I love our to and fro conversations and that we get to pause regularly together. Thank you for all that you do for the power of story and especially for your friendship.

My sister Emma, You are always there, you have always been my biggest supporter. I want to pause to acknowledge you, no matter what you have going on in your life you still always show up and give your best to those you love. Thank you for being you sis. I love you.

To my authors! This is for you! When you take a moment to master the Power in the Pause, you will experience a whole new level of success. The power of the pause allows for divine timing and in that divine timing all your dreams manifest, one by one, so that you can experience them fully. Ahhh, relax, pause and let the magic land right on time. Thank you for trusting me to be part of your journey. It is my joy.

A?K TV

We started A?K TV because we are ridiculously curious about life being utterly spectacular!

We believe that crafting the right question brings forth the right next step. Life is about deciding something, anything, and seeing where it leads you. We have to make choices. And to make great choices, we believe the ASK invites the outcome. Are you curious? Ready to dive in? What if you enjoy it? What if it makes you laugh and frees up your mind? What if we help you get closer to the things you really want to experience?

Who knows? We might just be the right answer.

www.ingramcontent.com/pod-product-compliance
Lightning Source LLC
Chambersburg PA
CBHW042319090526
44583CB00025BA/3206

*9 7 8 1 7 6 4 0 4 5 3 8 4 *